The
History
Worker

The History Worker

Jenny Drai

Black
Lawrence
Press

Black
Lawrence
Press

www.blacklawrence.com

Executive Editor: Diane Goettel
Book and cover design: Amy Freels
Cover art: "BLAST", encaustic, mica and oil paint on pine, by Valyntina Grenier

Published 2017 by Black Lawrence Press.
Printed in the United States.

CONTENTS

reader, a frame   I

First Glance   6

Hearst Castle Lullaby   9

The History of Character   12

The History Worker   19

Hearst Castle Lullaby II   20

Hearst Castle Notebook I [San Luis Obispo Mission Aside]   21

Chumash Highway Daydream   22

Hearst Castle Notebook II   26

The History Worker   27

by the book [1]   28

by the book [2]   31

The Discovery of America   32

Other Countried [for C]   37

The History Worker   39

The Objection of History   40

by the book [3]   42

by the book [4]   44

by the book [5]   47

The History Worker   48

Close the Book. Listen.   58

Acknowledgments   59

reader, a frame

George Hearst lived from 1820 to 1891 and struck it rich on silver mining. His only child, the newspaper tycoon William Randolph Hearst (W.R.H.), lived from 1863 to 1951. Moorish stars have eight points and decorate many of the medieval Spanish ceilings of W.R.H.'s Hearst Castle, now a California state park. (As a rule, the building contains artifacts—everything from furniture to fireplaces—obtained from the grand old houses of Europe, purchased after WWI when Europeans needed cash to rebuild.) Hearst Castle stands on land originally purchased by George Hearst in 1863. In its heyday, the castle included a zoo.

The Chumash are the people native to San Luis Obispo County in California, where Hearst Castle is located.

Bleuets is French for blueberries and is often printed on the grocery store label of that food product.

A *fata morgana* is a mirage of the appearance of water (although this usually refers to a vision of water in the desert).

The Plantagenet dynasty takes its name from the Latin for the common broom plant. (I was raised on stories of English history, not tales from this country's western expansion, and the personage of the historical Richard III was my first introduction to what might be termed 'the complexities of human character,' a theme I would return to as I considered various character assessments of George and W.R. Hearst.)

Hearst Castle includes two magnificent swimming pools, the outdoor Neptune pool and an indoor pool modeled after a Roman bath.

Deadwood aired for three seasons on HBO from 2004 to 2006 and includes a highly unflattering characterization of George Hearst. In that television program, Al Swearengen is the name of the fictionalized real-life saloon owner who carries out a murder at Hearst's behest and Seth Bullock is the town sheriff, also a real-life character, albeit in the series something of a tortured soul.

Legend has it that Richard III fought bravely until his end at Bosworth Field where Shakespeare has him cry, "A horse! A horse! My kingdom for a horse!"

Marion Davies, a silver screen comedienne in her own right and the girlfriend of W.R.H., lived from 1897 to 1961. Upon his death, she returned to his family the sizable share in his company that he had left her.

Richard III is the hero of several novels. Anne Neville was his wife.

Titus Flavius Josephus is the name of a Jewish historian who was born roughly in year 37 of the Christian era and who wrote of the crucifixion of Jesus of Nazareth by the occupying Romans. As a young child in parochial school, I first turned to my father's set of the 11-volume *The Story of Civilization* (Volume II, *Caesar and Christ*) to bridge religious insistence with some notion of historical possibility.

The Story of Civilization covers western history for the layperson and was published between 1935 and 1975, written by Will and Ariel Durant.

Indian casinos, like all casinos, include slot machines. Tribes pay revenue on what they earn from gaming and have to negotiate with states to open casinos.

In discussing whether or not alien life forms visiting our planet would be friendly, Steven Hawking has said, "If aliens ever visit us, I think the outcome would be much as when Christopher Columbus first landed in America, which didn't turn out very well for the Native Americans." (Huffington Post, updated 3/23/11.)

Columbus arrived in the Americas on October 12, 1492.

The Vikings arrived in the Americas as early as the 900s (and referred to the native people as 'Skraelings'—in modern Icelandic this word means 'barbarian' or 'foreigner.')

The *Star Trek* franchise presents an idealized and mostly enlightened view of a possible future in which Earthlings interact with alien life forms from other planets. *Falling Skies* aired from 2011 to 2015 and presents a decidedly bleaker view of what might happen if aliens came to Earth. The show makes repeated allusions to the American Revolution and in the end, with the help of some friendly aliens, the citizens of Earth defeat their alien overlords. *V,* (where "V" is for "Visitors") has been broadcast in many iterations over the years and involves reptilian aliens in human skin suits.

The "Trail of Tears" refers to the forced relocation of certain Native tribes in 1838 from their ancestral lands to Indian Territory.

Arad, from where my paternal grandfather's family emigrated, is a city in Romania. My mother's family comes from various regions in Germany. Prussia is in northeast Germany, Swabia in the south.

The Romanian Revolution took place in December of 1989 and resulted in the overthrow and death by firing squad of the Communist despot Nicolae Ceauşescu (referred to as Nicolae Caligula in the poem) and his wife Elena. Cluj is a city in Romania.

On the day after 9/11, the headline of the French newspaper *Le Monde* translated as "We Are All Americans Now."

Poulet is French for chicken.

Edward was the son of Richard III and Anne Neville. He died young, predeceasing his parents. The Woodville faction refers to the family of Elizabeth Woodville, the wife of Richard's older brother Edward IV, the father of the two princes in the tower.

The opening paragraphs of Wolfram von Eschenbach's *Parzival*, usually dated to the early 1200s, include a description of the moral character of man as mixed as the plumage of a magpie. A magpie has both black and white feathers.

Centurion is a 2010 film that depicts the Roman occupation of Britain. The film portrays native Britons defending their homeland and attempts to explain the fabled disappearance of Rome's ninth legion.

The artifact, this mind, pushes through.

First Glance

[1.]

it begins as George
'the boy the earth talks to'
hears silver ore   loss-glee
flying
heart artifactual gathering
retention   gather   collection
      sings his William
is a lately 8-point Moorish
         stars all over ceiling
streaking this land of many
changing hands   rich man's
zoo remnants   Goofus,
the firm white   northern bear
Indian deer   hart of Europe
buddies of cows, these
wildness zebras

[2.]

shell bead money   'discovery'
Conquistadores and smallpox
        the blazing state
            golden   sun bleaching
those loping   swaying
windswept grasses
the land as palimpsest
[descriptions written over their own blood]
[Tears for Fears at the Chumash Casino]
George Hearst's head of acreage
        cattle   grazing
William Randolph's   'I would like
to build a little something'
have built   have bitten
        off the alphabet of Amazing to record
a previous place's   tyranny of provenance

[3.]

hadn't thought of breakfast
all these books
    toast not egg
later was hungry   wanted porridge
served in vaulted rooms
the container of a deceased man's intellect
    the vault is air in the predilection of memory
all sealed up and let out   yes, please I touch
museum artifact   alarm-wired carpet
        not with fingers but with two blue
    eyes   is written
therein being reversal
revision   dearth   alteration
    gilt-books
pages lining a study
wanted porridge in that study with *bleuets*
    stirred into warm oat

Hearst Castle Lullaby

[1.]

had swum
had toweled off
like reading love
under an oaken tree
songs of Provençal
then squabbling because the chicken
breasts had not been thawed
of their ice raiment

[2.]

'amidst' as one known
language   such as never being *through*
[other more painful
versions of that definition—
tears salting the coffee]

no one could know where she walked
her glass feet

                              slight funk
of the Roman pool
green in this light this water
          agate   corporeal
unavailable

fata morgana

[3.]

the cold blue surface
had swum   had toweled off
[saying 'that' already]
to dismantle what's personal
magnified   dismantled   broken through
[lost glass that one could gather   precipitous]
above   beyond   below
            cavernous prepositions

and then I
closed my eyes, lay
me down

The History of Character

[1.]

fog in seams
      lessons are shouting
whom you love as the possibility of fact
girl, you sat   say it   *Indian style*
      what you desire is marvelous
sewing
or, how the deep past *smells*
      [tastes   mea culpa   to peer in those
eyes]
had you eaten the orange you would
      not pierce it cloven   hung on ribbon
to aromatize a foul-smelling world
      fog in ripples and cleaves
olfactory sense of nearby
salt in sea   it is true what you admitted

[2.]

as a child you lay on wood-
		slat flooring
a house carved out about your inquiry
			wanting to smell the sprig of broom
planta genista
Richard twisting nervous his ring
but knowing all the same
outcome of a murder
		as if pure good, pure evil
[George Hearst in *Deadwood*]
[G.H. in a propaganda film—*HEARST CASTLE*—
the building of a dream—
(voice booms)]
ever displaces gray
			[the evolution of Al Swearengen
		begins with swarthy swagger,
who kills and kills again but fears the final stain			:
					he mops up
				some sweet
			whore's blood]

[3.]

what I shall wear
anyone's silk guess
along this moon of cutlery
      moonlight   :   cutlery
the chattel of evening
      description of periphery
blasé   put upon   carefree
      jocularity
if I   pray subjunctively
this soup of should
      could broth had only   :   delirious would
have brushed an arm in love's
live scope   poor
Richard thwarted by no kingdom's
      horse   Marion
the guide says   *first screwball*
      comedienne
gives upon Hearst's death
his money back as proof

[4.]

Richard's imagined purity
    dear Anne
the romance writers type
full stoppages   brimming
supposition, tells the child
in the father's
room
historical gates
    gray dusk of a golden
heart is also glaucous   as a bloom
              on old red
        grapes reimagines morality
    do nothing
the child reads of Josephus
    story of the Nazarene
    commit treachery
breed heart you're lovely

[5.]

warm floor
abide my throat   ululate the proper
note   most suitable past
:   history coats me   :
charges in tandem
unhanded   all-burdened
along ridges of eyes
        The Story of Civilization
preciously 'where'
Will and Ariel Durant
        hide   'men of their times'
        what a child comprehends
squashed between
the bed   :   that wall

[6. *the general to Seth Bullock: 'we all have bloody thoughts'*]

crisp   bejeweled
low-hanging fruit
           monstrous pluck
evening fisticuffs unwind obedience
or refer to salacious
rumors   some violence
totem devoid of its shaman   Seth
           alight with   pounding pulse
unwinds shame   blue guilt
bends correctly

[7.]

Josephus' incarnadine
      aisles of type   perhaps one
      thinly scripted page
quakes girl's
      mind
      heart
      recessive blue eye   :   to read
who was?
is cutting   to burst the closed
book's paper boundary
character flows like script   the smallest
      fingers, this
heated house
who studies bluely characters
who were these men dying?   Lenten snow
first strike heart gold

The History Worker

deeply laden
       tureen of tumbling
star-mouthed
       platter of duck
or what one eats
in those rich houses
       esophageal history
eaten-bit story
producing an artifact
       previous of nothing

Hearst Castle Lullaby II

swam 10 laps   toweled off
as drink bespoke a tremor in one hand
       dove lovely   pike press into hilted
       air a wet wrung thing
had eaten   thus wiped a mouth
       counted 30 cement stairs
touched lime wash poured   etched as stone
who divides me   division
who devises   could be planes of light
          sidling through low
       cushions of night

Hearst Castle Notebook I
[San Luis Obispo Mission Aside]

as an adult this girl has quarters in her pocket but doesn't
fish them out for the tin-box 'donation' at the mission toilet
    :   she steps through the world of growing
roses, crosses grass lawns with loping dogs and straying
children   :   to be a tourist in her own state
:   everyone coagulates   :   Al,   Seth,
Jesus, Richard, George, William   :   at first in the
quaint photo she held the books upside down   :
also, learning the history of kings and queens from
Shakespeare   :   here is your father, reading, he is
shy and muddled   :   but flame   :   but
a candle never guttering   :   curiosity   proffered,
bound in love, like central things   :   although there
is rape and cruelty on all pages of history, she still learns
nuance   :   learns passing-down   :
    the artifact not as mace, goblet nor inlaid walnut
ceiling carved with Moorish stars   :   but
through hand, of *land,* a breakfast tea of motives never
supercilious to result

Chumash Highway Daydream

[1.]

says the Indian casino's
historical you-purge:
T gives the belt
          then takes back   hole-punched
leather   says T's father   *Indian giver*

breathing   exchanging
long lace of the highway
mist feet carbureting miasma
records the 'you'   cumbersome
token-pocket   pulling for pine-
apples, whatnot, rows
of cherries

[2.]

driving with relatives
                [with opinions]

who ought to pay
a lien to the future
turns down circuitous
unpaved lanes of unbent taxation

but didn't hear ice cold
swims tea in cobalt glasses
            not guilt but a day
'they don't pay'
she says
[the Mono tribe near Yosemite]
opens
rude loss

[3. *first contact*]

a recognition of distance
'discovers' our world
sleep paralysis   experimentation on nostrils
cold spoon fright
therefore colonization
therefore colonize
who are settled upon
[map dots]
pods in skies
the three encounters of mankind
[visitors in ships]
who are settled upon
[Apache, Comanche, Seminole, Sioux]
maybe not *Star Trek*   maybe *Falling Skies*
          without the happy end
and rub your eyes

then drive to La Cuesta Entcantade [Hearst Castle—the
enchanted hill]—in skin like tanned alabaster Romanian milk
past the green roadway sign [Chumash Highway]

where you
stem from
is not here

your life collects in what heart you choose   :
walks across the moral conundrum of two separate tours
            :   Marion loved him, she was 'the first
screwball comedienne'   :   or cute blonde young
trash breaking a marriage   :   how   you
contain your life as the crux of perceive   :   the
first guide loves her, puts on this fawn glove   :

        also, someone asking about the great stone fireplace
lilted out of a French dream   :   cream in your
tea   :   never lemon   :   the second guide
is not frivolity   :   whom broken   :

        who over a knee sends some cosmic spanking
        :   little Marion like a naughty kite   :
        gaze-traipsing   :   no   one   asks   about
ghosts

The History Worker

low orange globe
sun's ghost-in-the-view
saddled sideways
need not be folded
      neither diptych nor triptych
viewed as seams sewing
seascape says wine-dark
      azure   wine-dark
the precise room in which you stand, the carpet here,
un/splitting eras into co/existing entities
      all-between   some-light
lingered land to sea   looked
upon the future   not knowing
              eyes or hooks
    tincture spending raiment
unhands emotional   broom straw
swept apart of its own one swept part
wave unmuddled but there   this distance
        does and does not
     broach
   sweet ambassadors

by the book [1]

had so felt   :   in authenticity

:

[to grasp explanation explores mendacity]

:

had once lived   :   still do in a sheave of coal-black
spades

:

[not a deck of cards but a system of categories]

:

what it means to be 'historical'

:

[a person, within history, which describes impervious braces]

:

so done up   :   rendered flat   :   easily

:

to restore 'personally' the manifestations of memory and of
history

:

[your breathtaking, habitual taking of your leave, which reads
         not according to a book but to the facility to
         perceive]

:

told the hellions   :   told the bruises

:

[how one inadvertently remains in accordance with procedure]

:

if you mention *it*   :   *that* was the crux

:

[what it means to address identity]

:

one aspect   :   this—*say it*—key

:

the accumulation of history into the ability to speak

:

I had to   :   had to look at staircases

:

[individually or collectively]

:

or note breezes   :   the light flapping of coats

:

[in time, as an illness cures its own singular disease]

:

peered out   :   saw bright arms reaching

:

aboard me now comes no longer   :   oh sweet

:

other moon summer things marking the clock like pomegranate
seeds

:

according to the presence of small eventuality

:

learnt-bent   :   also seeds

:

in craving   :   I receive   :   historical time-stamp

:

bites up my teeth I say you probably

by the book [2]

for a swept time. bewildered by trees. if your—

I, my, mine, me—

skin isn't marked but still a difference. so skin. a light on skin.
she said you were bravely facing strewn codes. she meant. 'blush
on the permanent idea of roses.' as always new are growing. what
you want to be angry about so you're angry about something
else, which is a good reason to be angry anyways. oh sweet
things, stop cutting these loud trees! what you are *hurt* by, which
is more difficult than other forms of righteousness.
this is like a scream.
like a low tunnel and the momentary absence of light.
when I woke from the dream, there were fir trees on all sides,
and other green growth, grasses and such. that tunnel came
upon me like a white cloud of fog.

The Discovery of America

[1.]

shipwright dawn gray
wet mist
      sky-allele   rubbed
wrong friction stems of calloused palms
way along   is boating
tiller-love / adoration of star-
board   some European
idea of first
       braces of dates
    12. October. 1492.
like π, notation
indicates a never-end
race to 'new'

[2.]

in this pitching forward
          what-you-learn-when
the mind also in grip of provenance
          if we all could
understand what it feels like to be occupied
[Apache, Comanche, Iroquois, Wampanoag]
these benevolent Visitors / our reptilian overlords
some fictional titillation or is this
          manifest
Columbus sailed the ocean blue
splitting skin suit open that nightmare again
whereas in *Falling Skies* the plucky Second Massachusetts
how narrative reflects discomfort or
          maybe just fantasy
ocean blue dreams the Viking
          New England styles   door painted red
had better not eat us out of fractured house
          settles the 'first' birth
[Snorri, the son of Thorfinn and Gudrid]
Europe-breath   this bawling, mewling, darling
child of adventurers and thieves
:   natives attack   return with a force

land of gooseberry ferment

[one of the fantasies   :
we are so powerful of course we'll take back Earth]

[3. *personal America*]

Ms. Draia, Ms. Draia
oh say can you see

road bends   curves
         away   sways
once more to sight's
clarity range

5-year-olds   lined up by height
12. October. 1980   white construction
paper sails emblazoned
         red with Spanish crosses
the Niña, the Pinta, the Santa Maria
         then a passage of grades   who lines up now
                         is anyone's bright guess
3 paragraphs   the Trail of Tears
         severance pedagogical

says the
accident gene child
furled and forth
born of bread and immigrants' boats

Prussia, Swabia, Austria-Hungary, England, Romania
breeds down time
to little Romania of Chicago
                              Gheorghe Draia=
        Maria Duscan
sired in Arad, Romanian city of river
        |

  George Drai
(newly-minted)   meets Lucille of the flower farm
                the USO dance
        own-edged, genetic
luck herself
how we heave land

Other Countried [for C]

to say 'the child'
the girl watching Revolution
unfold   Nicolae : Caligula
other family runs to the hills
but the girl's nose
['America the Beautiful']
as the only trace of her East-Europe
:   falling apart her the immigrant speaks
:   as phrases and gestures are
only one part of love   :
later Caligula propped
against his own brick wall for the international
photo opportunity   :
to say 'the child wore this photo like her own
genetic luck'
[the accidents of genetics, where her
birth lands her on earth]
to say 'the woman tried to understand the past
of another woman's life'
:   is love
:   is how love shades accountability and
luck and Western guilt
[the palace of birth as a talisman]
or a lot of noise today like bullets *popping*

speaks the memory of revolution / Romania /
December 1989
or, the goose pimples on the immigrant's arms
like love or a thing of beauty (to be rid of
constant danger)
unlike the story of the gate at Christmas when C wanted to go
                    'in this, the weather in Cluj'
wanted to go   *sweet Jesu*
caroling in eventual evening

The History Worker

the avatar
[vehicle of history]
a sweet and voyeuristic pickle
marathon of wick-light
          to punish illusion
'seemed like a good idea at the time'
to write about
          organization in *aspect*
as dithering as formula
filling out
the space in transoms   'your turn'
[an opening above a door]

The Objection of History

[1.]

dialect broken through
heft-logic   code of rooms
    assemblage of rich
cogency   catalogues the passing days
no countryman calls himself by another
country's name   bone, lymph, ligature
as exception is not rule
as event perpetrates a singular
chamber of the body
        'thou art'   the catalogue

[2. *to question what it means to be beleaguered*]

        called to   what?

say it   trace eye

hotel's white ceiling

the land will be a lake of justice

a djinn from a smashed glass   element bottles

        to deny a placement

           'We are all Americans…'

      [French lunacy—that was distance]

you could lose your house

nuance gambling   to use

     a word like 'unify'

blends the all-thing

by the book [3]

you cannot write about a life that is not yours
        unless you determine your factor of resistance
:

desire broke up the countenance party and transformed to whitish
clay
:

Cluj, a city far away, Arad not closer in this globe-light
:

what is nearer is the unmentionable traffic
:

the terrain of interloping interference, which breaks due
        process of one bird-egg-nest, robin-cracked, blue-shell
:

I have never come from anywhere but the middle of a country
:

saying 'middle'   :   meant 'outside'
:

peering down a lane of slate and shale, this *built,* this mortared
thing
:

outside a lake, the demon of history, one premonition of future
        precipice, a copse of arching willows
:

the demon drinks the lake as if the crisp blue

water bespoke the sweetness of an indefatigable text

:

visions of the future prevail

:

past elucidation of what is not just, are parts, is the pestle

by the book [4]

bent the chamber

:

smashed one lobe against dispersal of ideas

:

wanted to scream
plain, besotted versions of past
antiquity
       in place of personal truth

:

frustration accompanies a loneliness that cannot be seen

:

sometimes the feeling *that*

:

risky perpetuation of one story standing in for another, for
example
       the Christmas bullets in Cluj

:

whizzing
by not *your*
gated apartment Communist cinderblock
but *hers*, corporeal

:

'this mark cannot be seen'

:

against versions of the politic body

:

storms triggering   :   semblance of passing

:

tamps down   :   evacuation of an enemy

:

could have bricks or lamps to quell this shelling

:

to shine a bright light on the identity of the periphery

:

could be understood as such or not

:

could be written   :   or not, dictated

:

or not, story collecting in sponges, drowned in a white sink

:

it is not what happens to me but that I
                    come somehow to this arrangement
          [wish to join you]

:

not to trumpet experience but to justify
          personal definitions of haunting a precipice

:

haunting, as the story left unfolded, untold

:

woman of Cluj, wayfarer of the winding
          stairwell, fresh-scented dryer sheets

:

not wanting

to tell her *everything*   :   simply

to belong

by the book [5]

you're wandering, identification by proxy. what broke me also unbroke me. like a fever, rupturing the bold skin's cheek. bridle-haft. unable to speak. faked *this,* mistook frequencies. breached necessity as one manifestation of democracy, a stinking yellow puddle you poured onto a thin skim of water of violets. I've found your lair. hand. molded year-arc, I've found your manifest lair—

read like so many, I

drive stones kicking softly the curb

sometimes of indecent anger I read as your

butter melts in the pan, fries, little sizzles

should be called 'breakslow'

                    forms to heal scars

The History Worker

indentured lassitude
are minds these children
swam laps-grammar
toweled off

Hearst-land   heart of cattle
flash-light, all-color, bells of the casino's
green evocation of 'Chumash
Highway' sign

bleuets stirred in oatmeal
'...all American now'

the opening of the door was not to see the artifact. not to mark with crayon numbers individual segments of stone in the places for fire. how the fireplace in Hearst Castle sustained transportation. hewn apart / together once more again. but continuing to understand the provenance of land itself. paintings on the walls of missions. how the changing hands of the land wove knots / stories into grass. you could stop there—perhaps you thought you

might in this kindergarten
magic of how you
learned the documentation of discovery

look upon   your self
peering at obliviated hands
[perfume from a balcony below, drifting through an open
window]
prefix-light—
do you remember when discovery first
dressed itself in single quotes?

the opening of doors to a hallway, then a fork in the hall. no it is
not so. but rather a retracing of one's steps. scouring woodwork for
clues. if I come aboard me now, I will tear the route asunder. will
not. will. slow, incremental

[perfume leaking through the screen, sharp pain in the head]

accrual of mercies. never say *never* the arbiter says, having spoken,
having bled. the first clue was Richard, nervous, twisting his ring
in the portrait without physical lamentation. dragged across a
stage. this preoccupation with history, the study of morals.

'of their times'
is house-light banter
       supper cooking
poulet with Lawry's seasoned salt
[little girl reading between the wall and the bed]
to lose your son   faint Edward
       the peak of your life
[*sons*] *of York*
administrate north
kingdom   Richard justifies
murder as defense   Woodville factionalism

it was only that what once was learned, relearnt in nuance. not enjoying the chicken, which later that evening some girl cuts apart in pieces and hides in a solid mug brimming with cold milk. the milk takes on a specter, a skim of spices. too generic, this taste. here is what happens. the arrival of a multiplicity of reference. closing one book to leaf through thin pages of another. the villainy of Shakespeare's villains. who crushes the facial bones with pillows. who orders the act. sifting. stepping to-and-fro along the oft-trod paths until the doors blow wide from breezes swinging hinges in these eternal hallways. 'discovering' ephemera and substance.

juvenilia   historical
preoccupation with thieves
          abandoned children   lost wives
resting out the afternoon in sheltered
groves of birch, elm,
discontented
oak   plumage-
struggle
                    you, color-coded
black-white
feathered story of man's
in/decency   [von Eschenbach's magpie]
      is not good to love / this lack of ruth
wife in grove   narrative
itself   when the highwayman
boards your coach *you say*
'purchased' these   'paid in kind'
          no dastards but   *you took what once*
                                        was mine

somewhere off, Hearst's dachsund barks in a new dog's body.

instrumentation of caring for lawns. to be intelligent is to digress.

like all lamps lit up at once in an estimation of the space between

opposites. between sorrows. or, between various manifestations of

splendor, which dazzle but do not always *hold*

the line. hold the line
bellows the broad
captain   mist
leaks out sound   flame-brush
spills down hillsides / the film
on movies

perpetrates a clause
        bee-bonnet   honey-
movie   *also love*
finds the *Centurion* in his
Pictish injury   etymology of 'misc'   :
[later, when all is done, he lays upon the ground,
the beloved native woman]
to turn away from Rome   what was done,
                                is done / the cut-
                        out-tongued-
                    raped tracker
                            leads ninth   to hell

a record of the mind held by which idea

the idea supposes another chair at supper. pulled to the rim of the
white tablecloth, embroidered floral grace. once wiped fingers, an
age before napkins. once fingers wiping hair. is immaterial. is *such*,
or, how we learn. studying the secret education of sinners *she
whispers* through mesh grills. you / pure / you future heart. arrived
at by study. *oh* she says [I—tumbling out of Roman sheets to swish
up the Roman blinds—an idea pouring through sun-stream,
cloud-light] *there you are. you   :   garrison   :   you
        :   indefatigable vulnerability   :
slight sight
in this rainstorm, understatement maelstrom   :
you are what I sought for years*

Close the Book. Listen.

be your own damnation

be chassis / industry / chassis

says party-lady   :   mouth full of cheese

redemption not part   :   bargain-guilt

crumbs of brie   :   an other *thing*

'the laziness of the colonized'   :   she says, wiping her mouth

you had better lay out the blunted knives   :
                                        'if we teach the slaves to read'

a child screaming at the table but does not know it

and when she 'knows'   :   the pickle of knowledge

my country 'tis of thee, sweet land of liberty

which could be damnation, an etymology of liberty and who bides it

combing through arti*fact*   :   alright. a girl fades.

ACKNOWLEDGMENTS

Thanks to the editors of the following journals for publishing work from this collection: *American Letters and Commentary* ["Hearst Castle Notebook I [San Luis Obispo Mission Aside];" Hearst Castle Notebook II;" "The History Worker (indentured lassitude)"]; *Omniverse* ["by the book [3]"]; and *Everyday Genius* ["Hearst Castle Lullaby II"].

THANKS

To Steven Meredith, who, as usual, has provided immeasurable friendship and support, and who has ensured, over a number of years, that life is not really ever boring. Ha ha, Steven. I said boring.

To my parents, both of whom, in their own unique way, did all sorts of wonderful things to foster my curiosity when I was growing up. I am thinking, among other things, of those weekly trips to the town library that my mother organized (and further facilitated by helping to carry home stacks, and stacks, of books) and the example provided by my kind-of-a-history-buff father, who, on top of everything else, never seemed to worry that I might mess up his expensive books. *The History Worker* is for both of you.

To Mike, Nicole, Corinne, Charlie, Max, and Francesca Drai, and to Sammy, Linda, Carter, and Landon Fox. Family by birth, family by choice. (Also, being an aunt is one of the coolest things that has ever happened to me. Thank you to my nieces and nephews for accepting my "artsy" Christmas presents with genuine gratitude.)

To all my teachers and fellow students in the MFA program at Saint Mary's College of California, which is where I found myself when I first started figuring out this poetry thing. Some people say poetry can't be taught, but I think this must be untrue, because I learned so much from each of you, lessons that stick with me to this day.

To Lisa Ludden, Sara Mumolo, and Mary Volmer, with whom I have traded poems over the years and/or had good, important, sustaining chats about writing and all kinds of other good stuff. Friends, all.

To Lukas Champagne, who never fails to remind me of the value of embracing enthusiasm in daily life. An exuberant friend is a good friend to have. Thanks for being in my corner.

To Aneta Bobinska, Danica Christensen, and Irina Dumitrescu, who collectively make a foreign country feel like home and who occasionally explain to me how things work in this part of the world. *Vielen Dank.*

To Valyntina Grenier, for her beautiful painting, which graces the cover of this collection. "Blast" is an 8"x8" encaustic work, created by the artist in 2010. Learn more at valyntinagrenier.com. (Lady, we are doing it!)

Last but not at all least, thank you to all at Black Lawrence Press, especially to Angela Leroux-Lindsey for her editorial insight, and for being far more detail-oriented than I am, to Amy Freels, who always makes my books look good, and to Diane Goettel, for more than I can say.

Jenny Drai is the author of three collections of poetry, including *Wine Dark* (Black Lawrence Press) and *[the door]* (Trembling Pillow Press). Two poetry chapbooks have also been published. They are *The New Sorrow Is Less Than The Old Sorrow* (Black Lawrence Press) and *:Body Wolf:* (Horse Less Press). A novella, *Letters to Quince,* was awarded the Deerbird Novella Prize and published by Artistically Declined Press. Her work has appeared in numerous print and online journals, including *American Letters and Commentary, Colorado Review, Denver Quarterly, New American Writing,* and *The Volta,* among others. In addition, she was recently awarded the 2017 Gail B. Crump Prize in Experimental Fiction from *Pleiades Magazine.* She studied literature and foreign languages at Beloit College and received an MFA in Creative Writing from Saint Mary's College of California. She blogs about her current project (a novel about Beowulf, bees, and queens), neurodivergence, and transatlantic life, and posts photos from her travels at jennydrai.com. She lives in Bonn, Germany.